express yourself

Yes, you can have the luxurious accessories and décor you crave! That's because ***Exclusively You*** Mock Croc and Smooth Faux Leather panels and embellishments give you the ability to make super-chic creations at a fraction of decorator prices. Use them to highlight photo frames, boutique-style pillows, and wall décor. Fashion handy valet trays or a whimsical pair of goggle-eyed owls. Gift a friend with a stunning tote bag or photo album. Want to change things up? We've included exciting options for alternative materials and easy shortcuts. With ***Exclusively You***, you get more than just great style —you also get the fun of creating each unique design!

LEISURE ARTS, INC.
Little Rock, Arkansas

bird frame

Finished Size: 6½" x 8½" with a 4" x 6" opening

Please refer to Tips and Techniques, page 36, before beginning work on your project.

WHAT YOU'LL NEED:

- 1 sheet of Mocha Smooth Faux Leather – Item #28507
- 1 sheet of Cream Smooth Faux Leather– Item #28361
- 1 sheet of Tan Smooth Faux Leather – Item #28329
- 6½" x 8½" unfinished wood frame with a 4" x 6" opening
- Brown acrylic paint to match mocha faux leather
- Large darning needle, stylus, or toothpick
- Spray adhesive
- Glue

WHAT TO DO:

1. Paint the back and all edges of the frame with brown paint and allow to dry.

2. To make front cover, place the frame, front side down, on the wrong side of the mocha faux leather sheet. Trace around the outer and center opening edges. Cut out the front cover along the traced lines.

3. Following the manufacturer's instructions, spray the wrong side of the front cover with spray adhesive. Aligning edges, place the front cover on the frame. Smooth out any wrinkles or air bubbles.

4. Using the patterns, page 30, cut the following from faux leather sheets:
    - From cream, cut 6 leaves, 1 bird, and 1 wing.
    - From tan, cut 1 branch.

5. Arrange the cut pieces on the frame front. When satisfied with placement, glue the branch and leaves in place.

6. Glue the wing to the bird and then glue the bird to the branch.

7. Dry brush highlights on the branch, leaves, bird, and wing with brown paint. Use the darning needle, stylus, or toothpick to apply dots of paint to the bird to make feathers and an eye and to the leaves to make veins.

flower frame

Shown on page 3

Finished Size: 8" x 8" with a 4" x 4" opening

Please refer to Tips and Techniques, page 36, before beginning work on your project.

WHAT YOU'LL NEED:

- 1 sheet of Cream Smooth Faux Leather– Item #28361
- 1 sheet of Green Smooth Faux Leather – Item #28330
- 1 sheet of Mocha Smooth Faux Leather – Item #28507
- 1 sheet of Tan Smooth Faux Leather – Item #28329
- 1 Tan Smooth Faux Leather Flower Pin – Item #28315
- 8" x 8" unfinished wood frame with a 4" x 4" opening
- Cream acrylic paint to match cream faux leather
- Self-adhesive gemstones in assorted sizes from 1/8"- 1/4" dia.
- Spray adhesive
- Glue

WHAT TO DO:

1. Paint the back and all edges of the frame with cream paint and allow to dry.

2. To make front cover, place the frame, front side down, on the wrong side of the cream faux leather sheet. Trace around the outer and center opening edges. Cut out the front cover on the traced lines.

3. Following the manufacturer's instructions, spray the wrong side of the front cover with spray adhesive. Aligning edges, place the front cover on the frame. Smooth out any wrinkles or air bubbles.

4. Using the patterns, page 30, cut the following from faux leather sheets:
    - From green, cut 2 large and 2 small leaves.
    - From mocha, cut 3 small flowers.
    - From tan, cut 3 small flower centers.

5. Arrange the cut pieces on the frame front. When satisfied with placement, glue the leaves, small flowers, and small flower centers in place.

6. Remove the pin back from the flower pin. Glue the flower to the frame front.

7. Adhere one gemstone to each small flower center. Adhere gemstones around the flowers, as desired.

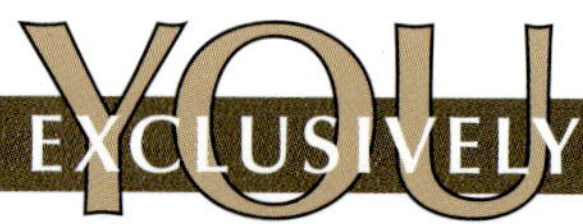

button pillow

Shown on page 7

Finished Size: 8" x 8"

Please refer to Tips and Techniques, page 36, before beginning work on your project.

WHAT YOU'LL NEED:

- 1 sheet of Copper Mock Snake – Item #28517
- $8^1/_2$" x $8^1/_2$" square of brown corduroy fabric for pillow back
- 1yd of $^1/_4$" (7mm) dia. decorative trim with a lip
- 8 brown $^3/_4$" (19 mm) dia. buttons
- 1 scrapbook brad of choice (we used a word)
- Polyester fiberfill

WHAT TO DO:

Match right sides and use a $^1/_4$" seam allowance for all sewing.

1. From Mock Snake, cut one pillow front $8^1/_2$" x $8^1/_2$".

2. To attach trim, matching raw edges and beginning near the center of one (bottom) edge, baste the trim to right side of the pillow front. Clip the lip of the trim as needed to make turning corners easier. When you reach the starting point, overlap the beginning end of the trim as shown in Fig. 1. Baste across the overlap.

Fig. 1

3. Spacing the buttons approximately 3" apart, sew the buttons to the pillow front. To attach the brad, cut a small slit in the lower right corner, slide the prongs through the slit and open.

4. Leaving an opening for turning along the bottom edge, use a zipper foot to stitch as close to the trim as possible to sew the pillow front and back together. Trim the corners.

5. Turn the pillow right side out and stuff with fiberfill. Hand sew the opening closed.

OPTION

Just imagine all the ways you could use this little pillow simply by changing fabrics and buttons! A sweet gingham or primary stripe pillow with novelty buttons would be a perfect addition to a child's room—you could even use individual letter brads to spell out a name! Add a little punch of color and fun to a mostly neutral room when you scatter several of these pillows, made from a bright fabric and embellished with funky buttons.

stamped pillow

Finished Size: 16" x 16"

Please refer to Tips and Techniques, page 36, before beginning work on your project.

WHAT YOU'LL NEED:

- 2 sheets of Mocha Smooth Faux Leather – Item #28507
- 2 sheets of Butterscotch Smooth Faux Leather – Item #28504
- 1 Brown Mock Croc Flower Pin Item – #28320
- 16½" x 16½" square of heavyweight decorator fabric for pillow back
- Rubber stamp (we used a large flower)
- StazOn® Timber Brown ink pad
- 1 brown 1¼" (32 mm) dia. button
- 1 brown ¼" (7 mm) square bead
- 16" x 16" pillow form
- Glue

WHAT TO DO:

Match right sides and use a ¼" seam allowance for all sewing.

1. From each faux leather sheet, cut one square 8½" x 8½".

2. Following manufacturer's instructions, stamp each butterscotch square as desired. Allow to dry at least 6 hours.

3. Matching raw edges, sew one butterscotch and one mocha square together to make Unit 1. Make 2 Unit 1's. Finger-press seam allowances open.

Unit 1

4. Placing colors opposite each other, match long edges to sew the 2 Unit 1's together to make the pillow front. Finger-press seam allowances open.

Pillow Front

5. Matching raw edges and leaving an opening for turning and inserting pillow form along the bottom edge, sew the pillow front and back together. Trim the corners.

6. Turn the pillow right side out and insert pillow form. Hand sew the opening closed.

7. Disassemble the flower pin. Discard the pin, inner petal layer, and flower center. Trim the ends of the middle and outer petal layers to appear less rounded, if desired.

8. Glue the middle and outer petal layers together; glue the button to the center. Sewing through all layers, sew the bead to the center of the button and flower. Glue the flower to the center of the pillow front.

OPTION

This two-tone Faux Leather pillow would also look fantastic if you used two coordinating fabrics. Try a print and solid, two high contrast solids, or a light and dark of the same color. Stamping on fabric is so easy, just be sure to look for ink that is designed for use on fabric. Finish your pillow by adding an embellishment such as a brooch, a doily, or a large button to the center.

family

clipboard art

Please refer to Tips and Techniques, page 36, before beginning work on your project.

WHAT YOU'LL NEED:

- 1 sheet of Soft Teal Smooth Faux Leather – Item #28360
- 2" x 2" square of Mocha Smooth Faux Leather – Item #28507
- Clipboard (we used a 6" x 9" clipboard)
- Rubber stamps (we used an approximately 1½" square dragonfly stamp and a swirl stamp)
- StazOn® Timber Brown ink pad
- Scraps of scrapbook or decorative paper
- 1 yd of ½" (7 mm) wide ribbon
- ½ yd of ⅛" (3 mm) wide ribbon
- Assorted embellishments (we used a tag, a sticker, beads, buckle, wire shapes, and brads)
- Glue

WHAT TO DO:

1. Draw around the clipboard on the wrong side of the soft teal faux leather sheet. Cut out the rectangle ⅛" inside the drawn lines.

2. Following the manufacturer's instructions, stamp the bottom half of the rectangle with the swirl stamp and then the dragonfly stamp using brown ink. To distress the edges, apply a small amount of ink to the edges of the rectangle and wipe away excess. Allow ink to dry for at least 6 hours.

3. From scrapbook paper, cut a 3" x 3" square. Distress the edges of the square with ink, if desired.

4. Remove the rubber stamp from its block. Trim away any rubber background, leaving just the shape of the dragonfly.

5. Arrange the paper square, faux leather square, and dragonfly in the center of the top half of the rectangle; glue in place.

6. Glue lengths of ½" and ⅛" wide ribbon across the rectangle just below the dragonfly. Add embellishments to ribbon and rectangle as desired. Cut the remaining ½" wide ribbon into 4" lengths and tie the lengths around the clip of the clipboard; trim ribbon ends at an angle.

7. Cover the tag with scrapbook paper and distress the edges with ink, if desired. Add beads, stickers, or other embellishments to the tag (we glued a length of ½" wide ribbon along the center of the tag and used an adhesive foam square behind our sticker to add dimension). Use ⅛" wide ribbon to tie the tag to the clip.

8. Center the finished rectangle under the clip on the clipboard; glue in place if desired.

wonder

coupon envelope

Finished Size: 8½" x 5½" (closed)

Please refer to Tips and Techniques, page 36, before beginning work on your project.

WHAT YOU'LL NEED:

- 1 sheet of Green Mock Croc – Item #28337
- ¼ yd of green jumbo rickrack
- Ka-Jinker® Quick-Click™ attachment tool
- Ka-Jinker® Felt Embellishment Set – Floral
- 3 hook and loop fastener dots
- Glue
- Liquid fray preventive

WHAT TO DO:

1. Slightly round the corners on one short end of the mock croc rectangle as shown in Fig. 1.

Fig. 1

2. Apply liquid fray preventative to the raw ends of the rickrack. Glue the rickrack to the wrong side of the short curved edge of the rectangle.

3. With the right side facing up, follow the manufacturer's instructions to use the Ka-Jinker to attach a leaf to the lower right corner of the rectangle. Layer, then attach an orange felt circle, a pink felt flower, and a round green Jem on top of the leaf. Attach a pink flower and a round green Jem to the top left corner (Fig. 2).

Fig. 2

1½"

2¼"

1"

1¾"

4. Matching wrong sides, fold the rectangle as shown in Fig. 3, forming a pocket.

Fig. 3

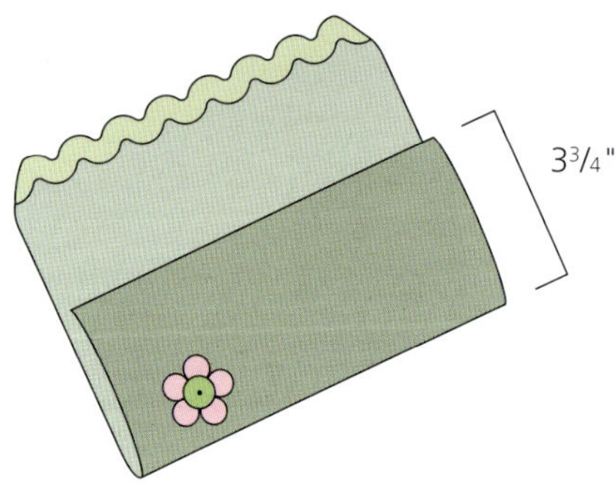

5. With the right side of the pocket facing up and backstitching at beginning and end of stitching, use a ¼" seam allowance to sew the sides together (Fig. 4).

Fig. 4

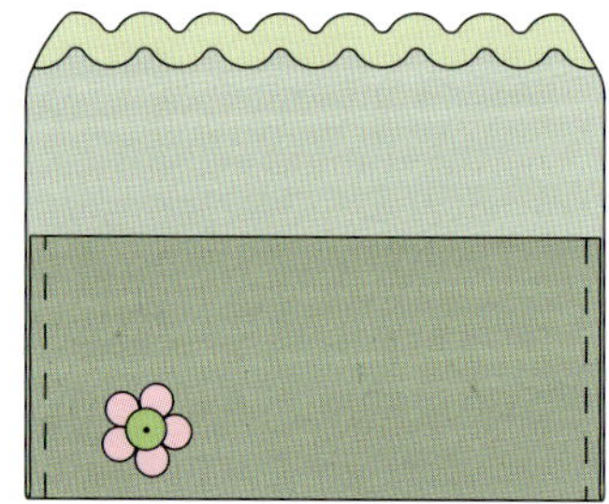

6. Fold the rounded end of the rectangle as shown in Fig. 5, to make the top flap.

Fig. 5

7. Spacing evenly, glue the loop fastener dots to the wrong side of the flap and the hook fastener dots to the right side of the upper edge of the pocket.

galvanized metal vase

Please refer to Tips and Techniques, page 36, before beginning work on your project.

WHAT YOU'LL NEED:

- 2 sheets of Cream Smooth Faux Leather–Item #28361
- 1 sheet of Copper Mock Snake – Item #28517
- 6 metal 3/8" (9 mm) square brads
- Metal embellishment (we used a word)
- 1 1/4 yds of 1/2" (7 mm) wide ribbon
- Galvanized metal vase (we used a 9" high vase)
- Glue
- Decorative edge scissors
- Tissue paper
- Removable tape

WHAT TO DO:

1. Determine which side of your vase will be the "front". To make the large label pattern, lay the vase down with the front facing up. Position a piece of tissue paper across the vase front; tape in place. Draw 2 lines across the vase from side to side 4" apart. Allowing for a 1" overlap at sides, as shown in the close-up photo on page 13, draw a vertical line at each side; remove the paper (Fig. 1). When laid flat, the drawn pattern will be curved (Fig. 2).

Fig. 1

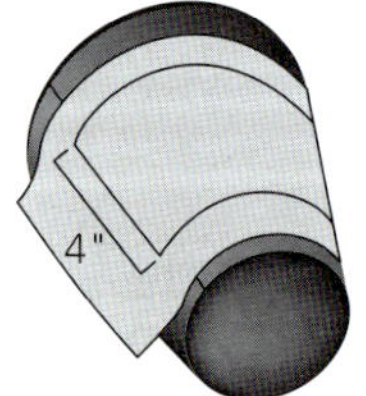

Fig. 2

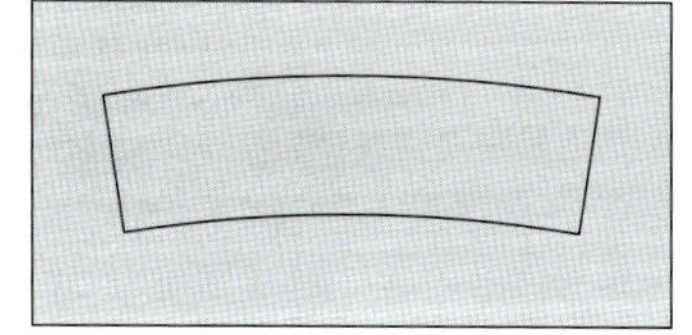

2. Cut out the pattern along the drawn lines. Wrap it around the vase to be sure it fits correctly; make adjustments if needed.

3. Trace around the pattern onto the wrong side of cream faux leather twice to make 1 front and 1 back large label. Use decorative scissors to cut out the large labels along the horizontal drawn lines. Use plain scissors to cut along the vertical lines.

4. To make the small label pattern, trim 1/4" from each long edge of the pattern. Repeat Step 3 using copper mock snake and plain scissors.

5. Use decorative edge scissors and the oval pattern, page 30, to cut one oval from cream faux leather.

6. Aligning side edges and centering vertically, glue a small label to the right side of each large label.

7. Tape one (front) label to the front of the vase. Tape the remaining (back) label to the vase, overlapping the side edges of the front label. On the back label, mark 3 evenly spaced dots 3/8" from each side edge for brad placement (Fig. 3). Use a craft knife to make a small slit at each mark through all the layers.

Fig. 3

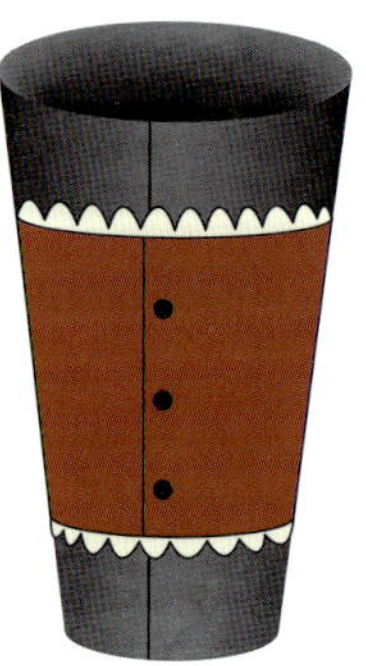

8. Fold the ribbon in half and make a small slit at fold. Aligning the slit on the ribbon with the center slit on the right side of the back label, insert a brad through all layers. Insert brads through the top and bottom slits.

9. Insert brads into all 3 slits on left side, cutting a slit in the ribbon to secure it with the middle brad. Tie the ribbon into a bow on the left side of the vase.

10. Center and glue the embellishment to the oval and then glue the oval to the center of the large label.

photo album

Finished Size: 8" x 8"

Please refer to Tips and Techniques, page 36, before beginning work on your project.

WHAT YOU'LL NEED:

- 2 sheets of Soft Teal Smooth Faux Leather – Item #28360
- 1 sheet of Scarlet Smooth Faux Leather– Item #28362
- 1 sheet of Mocha Smooth Faux Leather – Item #28507
- 1 sheet of Green Smooth Faux Leather – Item #28330
- 1 Tan Smooth Faux Leather Flower Pin – Item #28315
- 1 yd of 1/2" (13 mm) wide decorative-edge green ribbon
- 8" x 8" purchased photo album with plain covers
- 1/4" (7 mm) dia. hole punch
- 1/2" (13 mm) dia. circle punch (optional)
- 5/8" (16 mm) dia. circle punch (optional)
- Ka-Jinker® Quick-Click™ attachment tool, 3 small green flower-shaped Jems, and 3 black Links
- Spray adhesive
- Glue
- Tracing paper
- 1/2" (13 mm) wide double-stick tape (optional)

WHAT TO DO:

1. Disassemble the photo album and unfold the covers. Using the covers as patterns, trace around the album front and back on the wrong side of the soft teal faux leather sheets. Mark placement of holes for fasteners.

2. Cut out faux leather covers on traced lines and use the 1/4" hole punch to punch holes at marks.

3. Following the manufacturer's instructions, spray the wrong side of each faux leather cover with spray adhesive. Matching edges, smooth the faux leather covers onto the cardboard covers. Reassemble the album.

4. Using the patterns, page 30, cut the following from faux leather sheets:
   - From scarlet, cut 6 small circles and 3 large circles (or use circle punches).
   - From mocha, cut 1 of each vine.
   - From green, cut 4 leaves.

5. Disassemble the flower pin to make 3 flowers. Trim approximately 1/4" from the outer edges of the petals of the middle layer.

6. Arrange the leaves, vines, small circles, and flowers on the front cover. When satisfied with placement, glue the pieces in place.

7. Following manufacturer's instructions, use the Ka-Jinker to attach a flower Jem to each large circle. Glue the large circles to the center of each flower.

8. Tie the ribbon around the front cover. Use double stick tape to hold the ribbon in place, if desired.

tote bag

Finished Size: 16" x 15" x 2½"

Please refer to Tips and Techniques, page 36, before beginning work on your project.

WHAT YOU'LL NEED:

- 2 sheets of Black Mock Croc – Item #28335
- 1 sheet of Black Smooth Faux Leather – Item #28332
- 1 black Faux Leather-Grain Adjustable Handle – Item #28508
- 1 yd of black/white print fabric
- 1" silver swivel clasp – Item #28342
- 1 silver 1⅞" (48 mm) dia. decorative medallion
- ¼ yd of 1" (25 mm) wide black satin ribbon
- 17" x 24" rectangle of low-loft batting
- Glue

WHAT TO DO:

Use a ½" seam allowance for all sewing unless otherwise noted.

1. Cut the following pieces:
   - From black mock croc, cut 4 rectangles 5½" x 8½"
   - From black faux leather, cut 2 tabs 2½" x 5", and using pattern, page 30, cut 2 circles.
   - From black/white print fabric, cut 1 body 17" x 24" and 1 lining 17" x 29".

2. To make the tote, match raw edges and baste the batting rectangle to the wrong side of the body. Matching right sides and short edges fold the body in half and sew across both short edges.

3. To box the bottom, align the side seams with center bottom fold line; stitch across the point 2½" from the tip (Fig. 1). Repeat for the remaining end.

Fig. 1

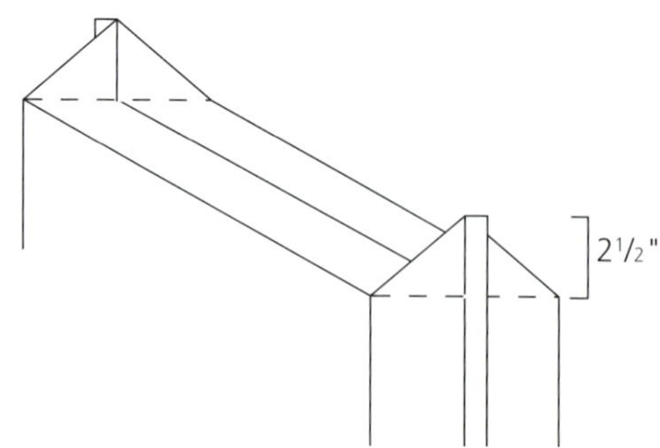

4. To make the tote trim, work from the right side to overlap the short ends of the mock croc rectangles ½"; pin. Zigzag the rectangles together along the overlapped edges forming a loop (Fig. 2).

Fig. 2

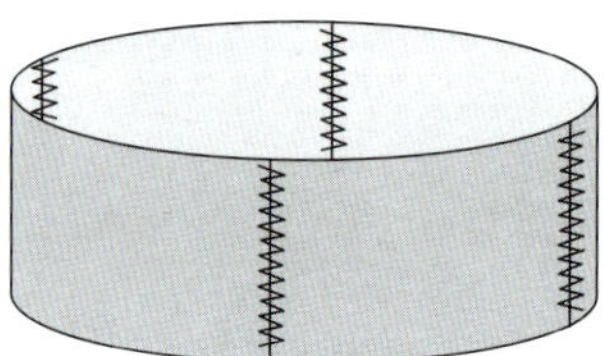

5. Matching right sides, raw edges and side seams, sew the trim and body together. Turn to the right side and finger press the seam allowances towards the body. Topstitch ¼" from seam on body.

6. For lining, match right sides and short edges and fold lining in half. Leaving an opening for turning in one seam, sew across both short edges.

7. Refer to Step 3 to box the bottom of the lining.

8. For tabs, fold each tab as shown in Fig.3 overlapping long edges 1/4". Centering overlapped edges at the back of the tab, zigzag down the center of tabs (Fig. 4).

Fig. 3

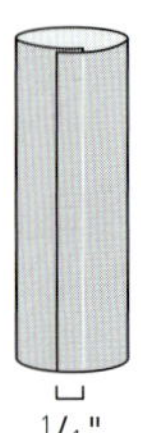

Fig. 4

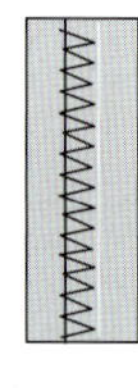

9. Matching short ends, place one tab through each handle ring and fold in half. Baste across short ends (Fig. 5).

Fig. 5

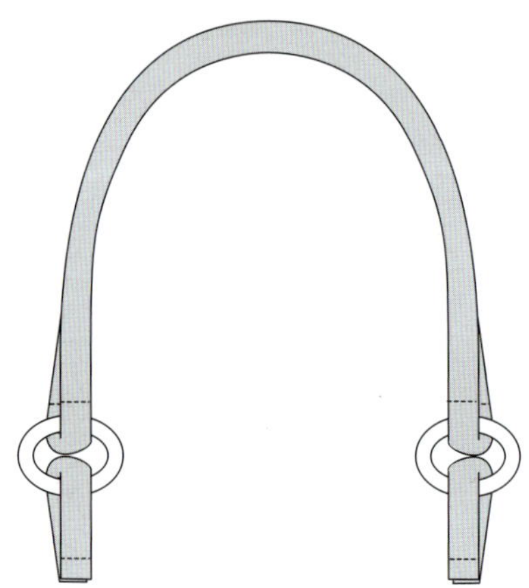

10. Matching right sides and raw edges, baste one tab to each side seam (Fig. 6).

Fig. 6

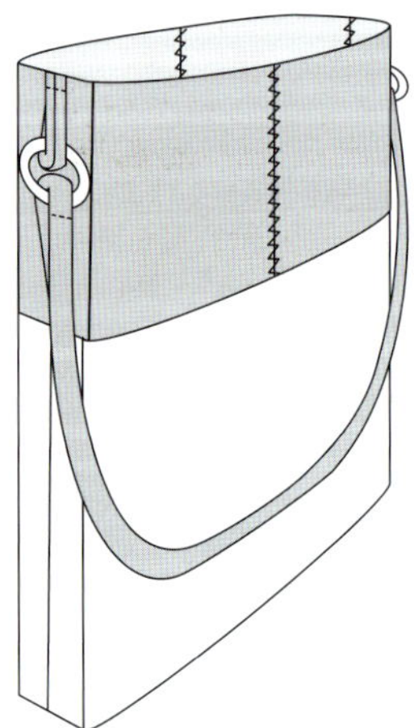

11. Matching right sides and raw edges, slip the tote inside the lining with the handle between the layers. Sew around the top edge through all layers. *Note:* Because you will be sewing through several layers at the side seams, you will need to sew slowly across those areas.

12. Turn the tote right side out through the opening and then push lining down inside of the tote. Finger-press the top edge of the tote to make the tote trim lay flat. Topstitch around tote 1/4" from the top edge.

13. Glue the medallion to the right side of one circle.

14. Matching raw ends, fold the ribbon in half over the loop of the swivel clasp. Matching wrong sides and sandwiching the ribbon between the layers, glue the circles together approximately 1/2" below the swivel clasp. Trim the ribbon ends as desired. Clip the swivel clasp to the handle.

OPTION

While the Mock Croc trim adds a sophisticated look to this tote, sometimes a girl needs a fun, funky bag, too. Choose two trendy fabrics and a coordinating Exclusively You handle. Instead of overlapping and zigzagging the trim, match right sides and use a 1/4" seam allowance to sew the rectangles into a loop. Use fabric to make the tabs for the handles then just follow the rest of the instructions for your one-of-a-kind tote!

owls

Shown on page 21

Large Owl finished size: 8" tall
Small Owl finished size: 6½" tall

Please refer to Tips and Techniques, page 36, before beginning work on your project.

LARGE OWL

WHAT YOU'LL NEED:

- 2 sheets of Tan Smooth Faux Leather – Item #28329
- 1 sheet of Navy Smooth Faux Leather – Item #28328
- 1 sheet of Green Smooth Faux Leather – Item #28330
- 1 sheet of Soft Teal Smooth Faux Leather – Item #28360
- 1 sheet of Cream Smooth Faux Leather – Item #28361
- 2½" x 4½" rectangle of orange felt
- Ka-Jinker® Quick-Click™ attachment tool, 2 small green flower-shaped Jems, and 2 blue Links
- Poly-Pellets®
- Polyester fiberfill
- Decorative-edge scissors
- Glue

WHAT TO DO:

Match wrong sides and use a ¼" seam allowance for all sewing. Always begin and end stitching with backstitching. Note: If you desire scallops on the back of the large owl, cut 2 of each scallop and attach them in the same manner as the front scallops.

1. Enlarge the patterns, pages 31-32, 121% and cut the following from smooth faux leather sheets and felt:
   - From tan, cut 2 owls (front and back), 1 beak, and 1 gusset.
   - From navy, cut 1 upper scallop and 1 foot.
   - From green, cut 1 middle scallop.
   - From soft teal, cut 1 lower scallop.
   - From cream, cut 1 eye background.
   - From orange felt, cut 2 eyes using decorative-edge scissors.

2. With right sides facing, position the bottom edge of the lower scallop ½" above the bottom edge of owl front; glue in place. Arrange and then glue the middle, and upper scallops, beak, and eye background to the front.

3. Topstitch around the eye background ⅛" from the raw edges.

4. Matching outer edges and dots, pin the front and gusset together. To sew the front and gusset together, start and stop at dots and taper the seam allowances to the dots on the gusset (Fig. 1).

Fig. 1

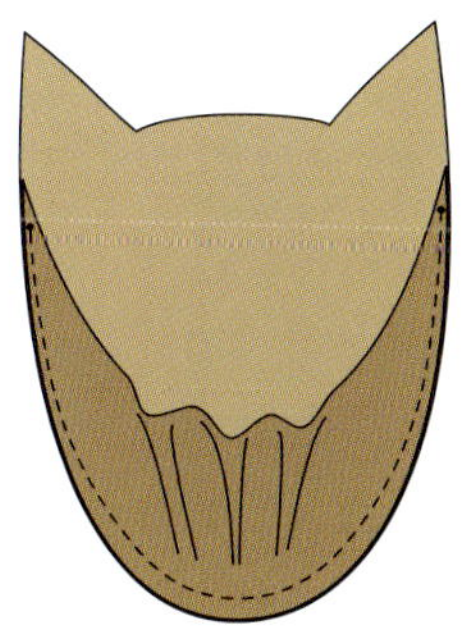

5. Matching outer edges and dots, pin the back and front/gusset together. Starting and stopping at dots and tapering seam allowance to the dots on the gusset, sew the back and front/gusset together. Leaving the top edges un-sewn between the ears, sew from the dots around the ears (Fig. 2).

Fig. 2

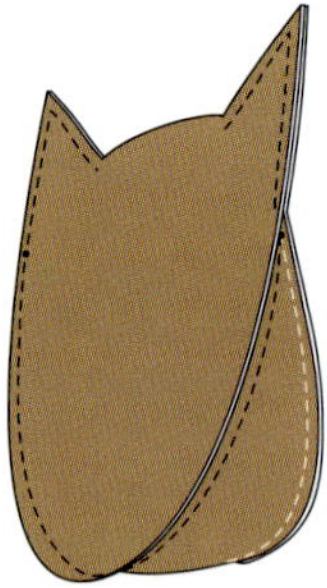

6. Fill the bottom of the owl with poly-pellets and then stuff the remainder of the owl with fiberfill Sew the opening closed (Fig. 3).

Fig. 3

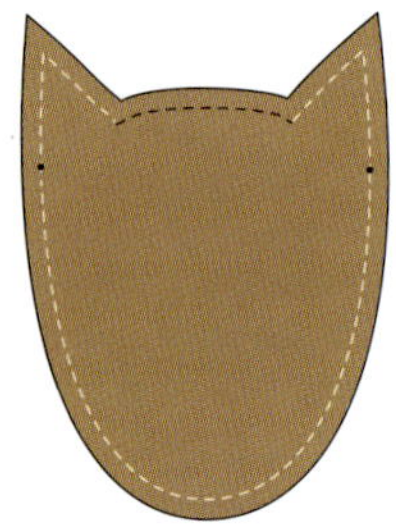

7. Glue the foot to the center bottom of the owl.

8. Following manufacturer's instructions, use the Ka-Jinker to attach a flower Jem to each eye. Glue the eyes to the eye background.

OPTION

Our wise owls, while definitely handsome in their Exclusively You Faux Leather and Mock Croc finery, would also be attractive made of felt. Because it has no right or wrong side and does not ravel, felt is a great option when making these birds. Using buttons for the eyes would make this project even faster and easier.

SMALL OWL

WHAT YOU'LL NEED:

- 1 sheet of Butterscotch Smooth Faux Leather – Item #28504
- 1 sheet of Berry Smooth Faux Leather – Item #28327
- 1 sheet of Scarlet Smooth Faux Leather – Item #28362
- 1 sheet of Pink Smooth Faux Leather – Item #28326
- 1 sheet of Cream Smooth Faux Leather – Item #28361
- Ka-Jinker® Quick-Click™ attachment tool
- Ka-Jinker® Felt Embellishment Set – Geometric
- Poly-Pellets®
- Polyester fiberfill
- Glue

WHAT TO DO:

Match wrong sides and use a 1/4" seam allowance for all sewing. Always begin and end stitching with backstitching.

1. Using the patterns, pages 31-32, cut the following from smooth faux leather sheets:
   - From butterscotch, cut 2 owls (front and back), 1 gusset and 1 beak.
   - From berry, cut 2 upper scallops and 1 foot.
   - From scarlet, cut 2 middle scallops.
   - From pink, cut 2 lower scallops.
   - From cream, cut 1 eye background.

2. Follow Step 2 of the Large Owl to glue the lower, middle, and upper scallops to the owl front *and* back. Glue the beak and eye background to the front only.

3. Follow Steps 3-7 of the Large Owl.

4. Using 2 aqua round felt disks and 2 green round Jems from the Ka-Jinker® felt embellishment set, follow Step 8 of the Large Owl to attach the eyes.

valet trays

Finished Sizes:
Woman's: 5¾" x 7" x 1½"
Man's: 5" x 7" x 1½"

Please refer to Tips and Techniques, page 36, before beginning work on your project.

WOMAN'S VERSION

WHAT YOU'LL NEED:

- 1 sheet of Purple Mock Croc – Item #28339
- 1 sheet of Pink Smooth Faux Leather– Item #28326
- 1 Pink Smooth Faux Leather Flower Pin – Item #28316
- 5¾" x 7" rectangle of mat board
- ¼" (7 mm) dia. hole punch
- 8 decorative brads
- Glue

WHAT TO DO:

1. Center, then glue mat board to the wrong side of purple mock croc sheet. With right side up, center then glue pink faux leather sheet to the top of the mat board.

2. Using a ¼" seam allowance, sew the raw edges together. Using a zipper foot and sewing as close as possible to the mat board, stitch around the mat board through both layers (Fig. 1).

Fig. 1

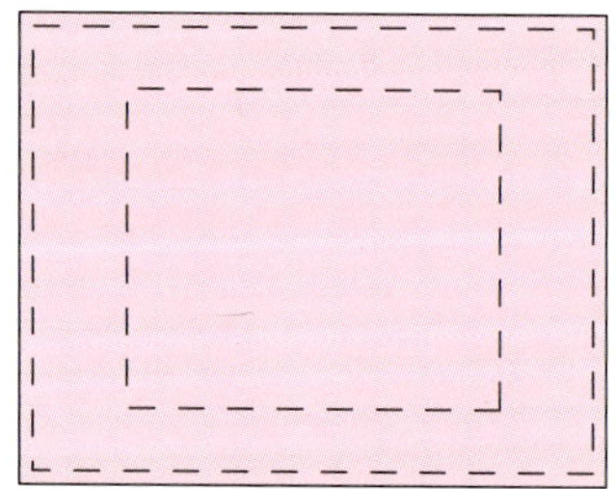

3. Referring to Fig. 2, place marks at each corner of the sheet. Punch a hole at each mark.

Fig. 2

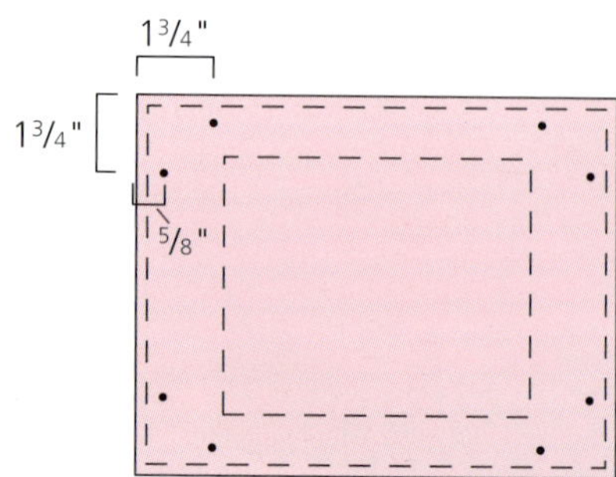

4. On pink side, apply a thin line of glue around each hole. Pinch one corner until holes align. Use a clothespin or paperclip to hold corner in place. Repeat for remaining corners. Allow to dry.

5. Insert a brad through the hole from the outside (purple side) in both directions. Fold prongs to one side to secure (Fig. 3).

Fig. 3

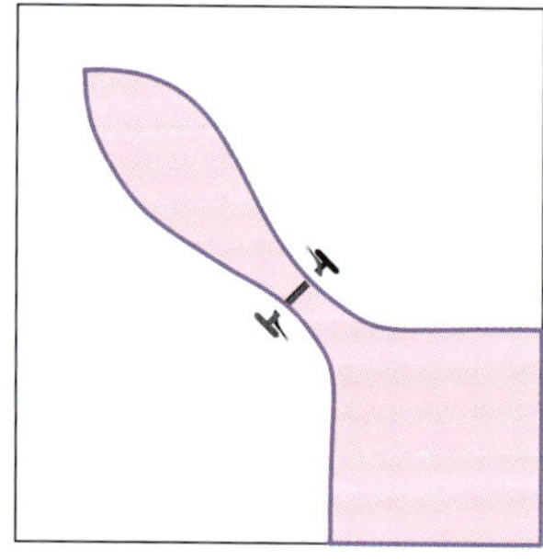

6. Remove the pin back and outer petal layer from the flower pin. Matching wrong sides, glue the outer petal and middle petals together. Glue the flower to one corner of the tray.

MAN'S VERSION

WHAT YOU'LL NEED:

- 1 sheet of Light Navy Mock Croc – Item #28334
- 1 sheet of Navy Smooth Faux Leather– Item #28328
- 5" x 7" rectangle of mat board
- 1/4" (7 mm) dia. hole punch
- 8 decorative brads
- Glue

1. Using light navy mock croc and navy smooth faux leather sheets and spacing holes as shown in Fig. 4, follow Steps 1-5 of the Women's Version to make the Man's Version.

Fig. 4

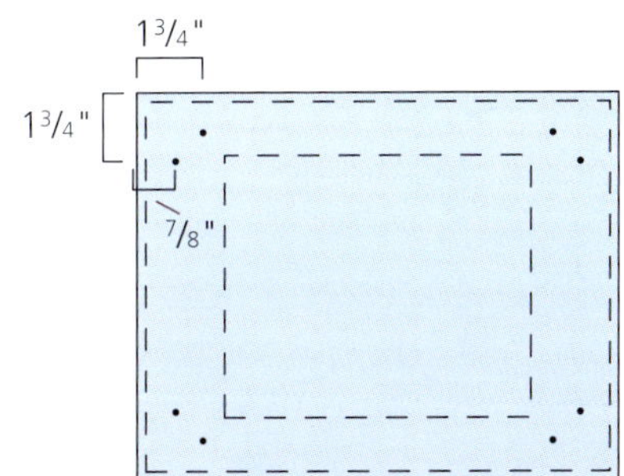

redbird

Finished Size: 5" tall

Please refer to Tips and Techniques, page 36, before beginning work on your project.

WHAT YOU'LL NEED:

- 1 sheet of Scarlet Smooth Faux Leather – Item #28362
- 1 sheet of Cream Smooth Faux Leather – Item #28361
- 1 sheet of Soft Teal Smooth Faux Leather – Item #28360
- Scrap of Butterscotch Smooth Faux Leather – Item #28504
- 1/4" (7 mm) dia. hole punch
- Polyester fiberfill
- Poly-Pellets®
- Glue

WHAT TO DO:

Match wrong sides and use a 1/4" seam allowance for all sewing. Always begin and end stitching with backstitching.

1. Using the patterns, page 33, cut the following from smooth faux leather:
    - From scarlet, cut 1 bird (front) and 1 bird reversed (back). Cut 1 gusset.
    - From cream, cut 2 small and 2 large wing scallops.
    - From soft teal, cut 1 tail and 1 tail reversed. Cut 2 wings and 2 wing scallops.
    - From butterscotch, cut 1 beak and 1 beak reversed.

2. For the beak, match wrong sides and raw edges to glue the beaks together. Repeat to glue the tails together. Punch holes where indicated on tail.

3. Matching outer edges and dots and tapering the seam allowances on gusset to the dots, sew the gusset to the front and then the back (Figs. 1-2).

Fig. 1

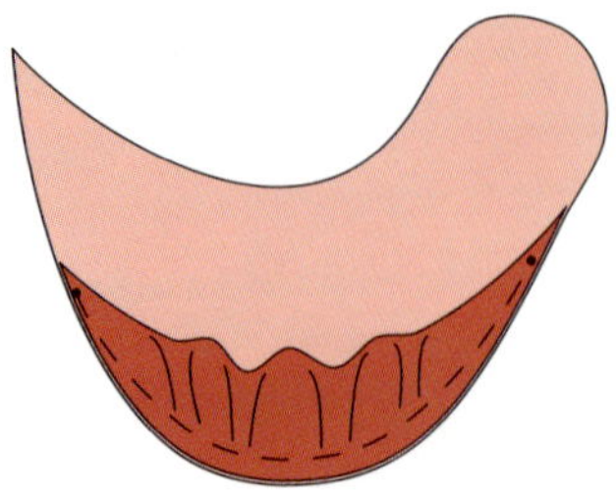

Fig. 2

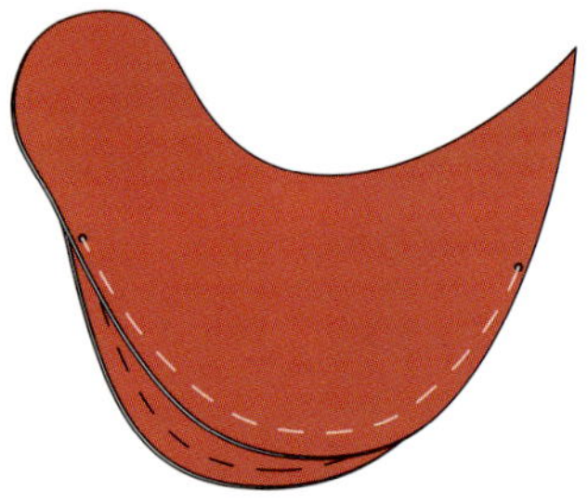

4. Matching outer edges, pin the remaining un-sewn edges of the front and back together. Pin the beak and tail between the layers where indicated by stars (Fig. 3).

Fig. 3

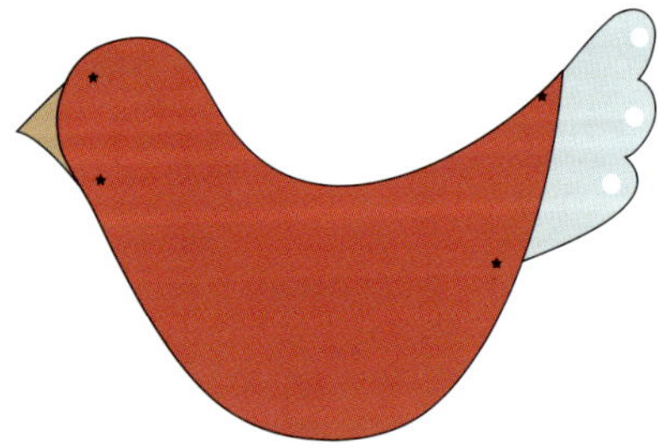

5. Leaving the top edges between triangles un-sewn for stuffing, sew the front and back together.

6. Fill the bottom of the bird with poly-pellets and then stuff the remainder of the bird with fiberfill. Sew the opening closed.

7. For the wings, punch a hole in the curve of each wing scallop. Reserve 2 holes to use for eyes.

8. Layer and then glue 1 wing, 1 large wing scallop, 1 wing scallop, and 1 small wing scallop. Make two wings. Glue one wing to either side of the bird.

9. Glue one eye to either side of the bird's head.

personalized tray

Please refer to Tips and Techniques, page 36, before beginning work on your project.

WHAT YOU'LL NEED:

- 2 sheets of Cream Smooth Faux Leather– Item #28361*
- 1 sheet of Black Smooth Faux Leather – Item #28332
- Unfinished wood tray (ours measures 8½" x 13" x 1½")
- Clear acrylic Plexiglas® rectangle to fit in tray bottom
- Black high gloss spray paint
- 3/8 yd of 1/2" (13 mm) wide ribbon
- Glue

* If your tray is larger than ours, additional faux leather and ribbon may be required.

WHAT TO DO:

1. Paint the tray and allow it to dry.

2. Measure the length and width of the inside bottom of your tray. Piecing as necessary and making sure seam(s) are placed where desired, cut the cream faux leather pieces to fit the tray bottom; glue in place.

3. Cut a length(s) of ribbon to cover the seam(s) between the faux leather pieces; glue in place.

4. To make a pattern for the monogram, use your home computer software to find and print an initial in the font of your choice. Our initial is 4" tall.

5. Using the patterns, page 34, and your monogram pattern, cut 1 of each pattern A-E and 1 initial from the black faux leather sheet.

6. Arrange the cutouts on the cream tray bottom. When satisfied with the arrangement, glue each piece in place.

7. Place clear acrylic rectangle in tray.

wall art

Please refer to Tips and Techniques, page 36, before beginning work on your project.

WHAT YOU'LL NEED:

- 2 sheets of Green Mock Croc – Item #28337
- 2 sheets of Copper Mock Snake – Item #28517
- 1 sheet of Maroon Mock Croc – Item #28338
- 1 sheet of Berry Smooth Faux Leather – Item #28327
- 1 sheet of Butterscotch Smooth Faux Leather – Item #28504
- 1 sheet of Cream Smooth Faux Leather – Item #28361
- 1 sheet of Green Smooth Faux Leather– Item #28330
- Turquoise acrylic paint
- Assorted rubber stamps (we used letters, a vine, a floral rectangle, and a postal mark)
- StazOn® Timber Brown ink pad
- StazOn® Saddle Brown ink pad
- 3 artist stretched canvases 8" x 10"
- 36" x 12" picture frame
- 9 round brads
- 1/8" (3 mm) dia. hole punch
- Glue

WHAT TO DO:

1. Paint the surface and sides of each canvas with acrylic paint and allow to dry.

2. With canvases horizontal, follow the ink manufacturer's instructions to stamp each canvas as desired and allow to dry. Note: We used Timber Brown ink for the floral rectangle and Saddle Brown for the remaining stamps.

3. Measure the depth of the canvas sides and cut 6 strips 10" x the depth measurement and 6 strips 8" x the depth measurement from green mock croc. Glue the strips around the sides of each canvas.

4. Using the patterns, page 35, cut the following from faux leather sheets:
   - From copper, cut 3 stems.
   - From maroon, cut 6 outer petals.
   - From berry, cut 6 middle petals.
   - From butterscotch, cut 3 buds and 6 inner petals.
   - From cream, cut 3 bud centers and 6 flower centers.
   - From green faux leather, cut 6 leaves and 3 leaves reversed.
   - From green mock croc, cut 6 leaves and 3 leaves reversed.

5. Cut out stamens along the detail lines on cream flower centers and punch holes where indicated on pattern.

6. Arrange the cutouts on the canvases. When satisfied with the arrangement, glue each piece in place.

7. To add brads, use a craft knife to cut a small slit in the canvas at the base of each flower and bud. Insert the prongs in the slits and open.

8. To display, hang the frame horizontally. Spacing evenly inside the frame, hang each canvas so that the canvases appear to "float".

OPTION

Customize this trio of wall hangings by using a soft tone-on-tone or muted print fabric to completely cover the canvases and eliminate painting, covering the sides, and stamping the background. To take it one step further, instead of Faux Leather, use your favorite method of fusible appliqué to make fabric flowers and stems from the patterns. Fuse the pieces to your fabric-covered canvases. Stencil, stamp, or paint the words and your wall art is finished!

BIRD FRAME

FLOWER FRAME

PHOTO ALBUM

TOTE BAG

GALVANIZED METAL VASE

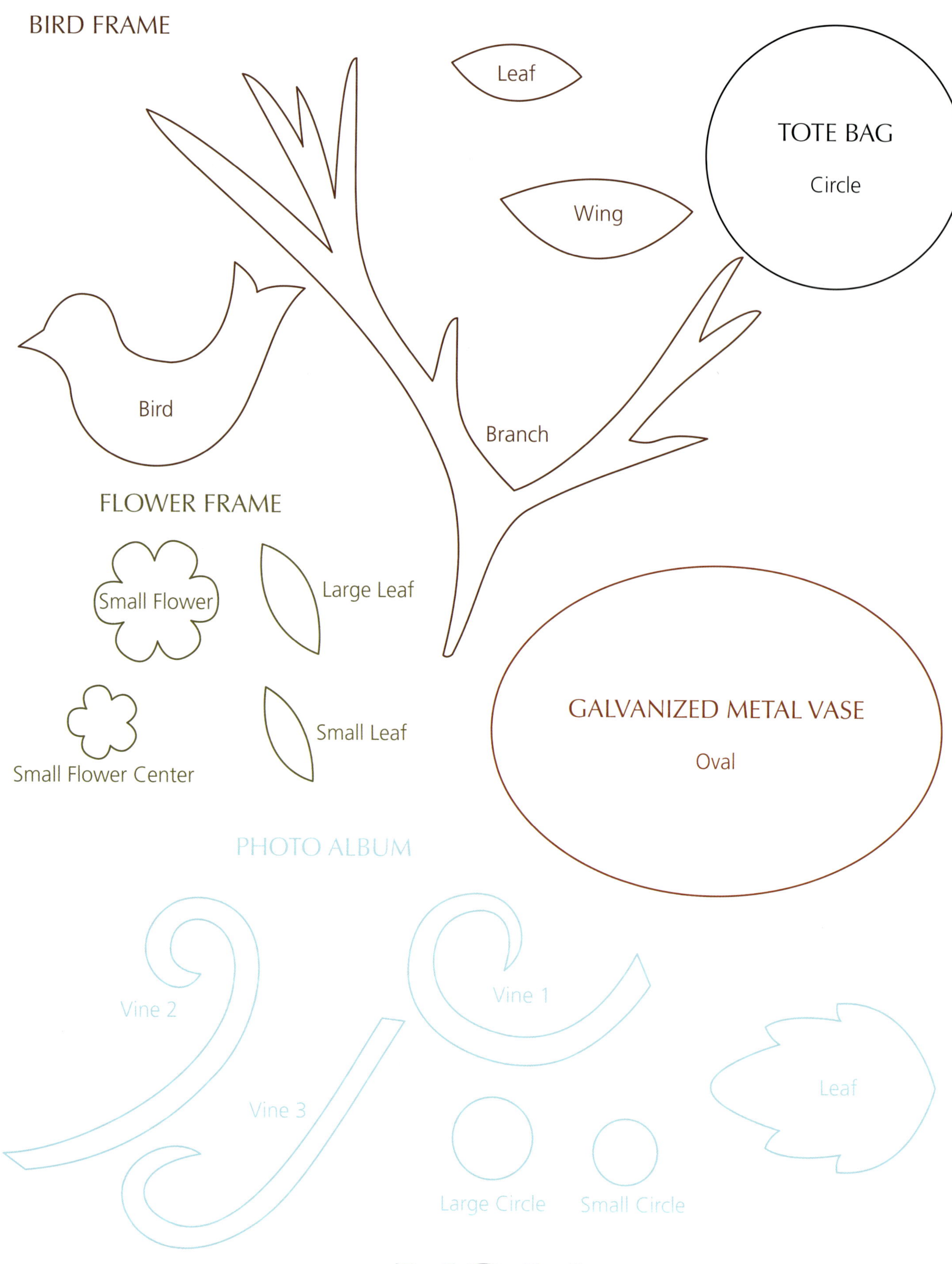

OWLS

For Large Owl, enlarge patterns 121%.
For Small Owl, use patterns as printed.

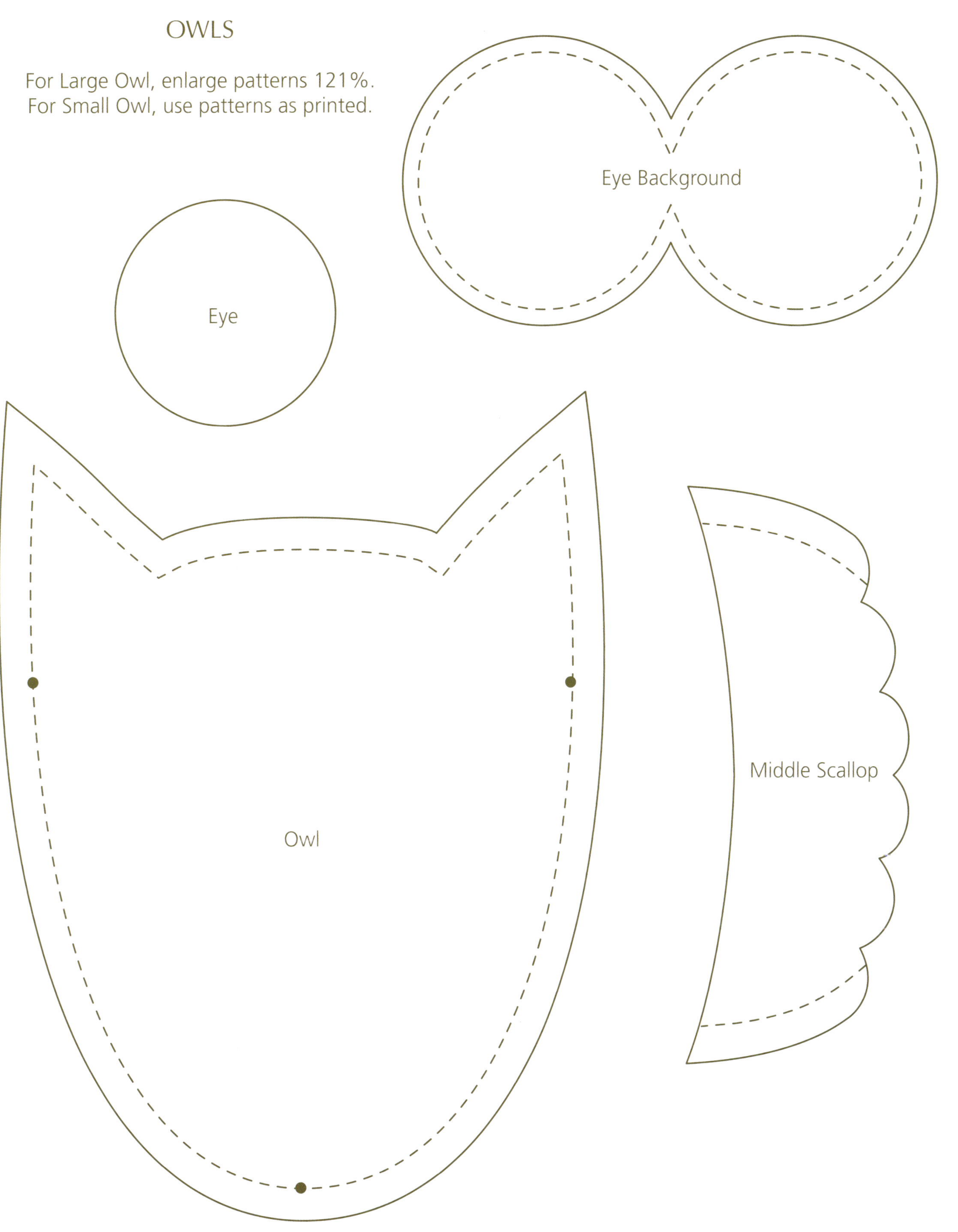

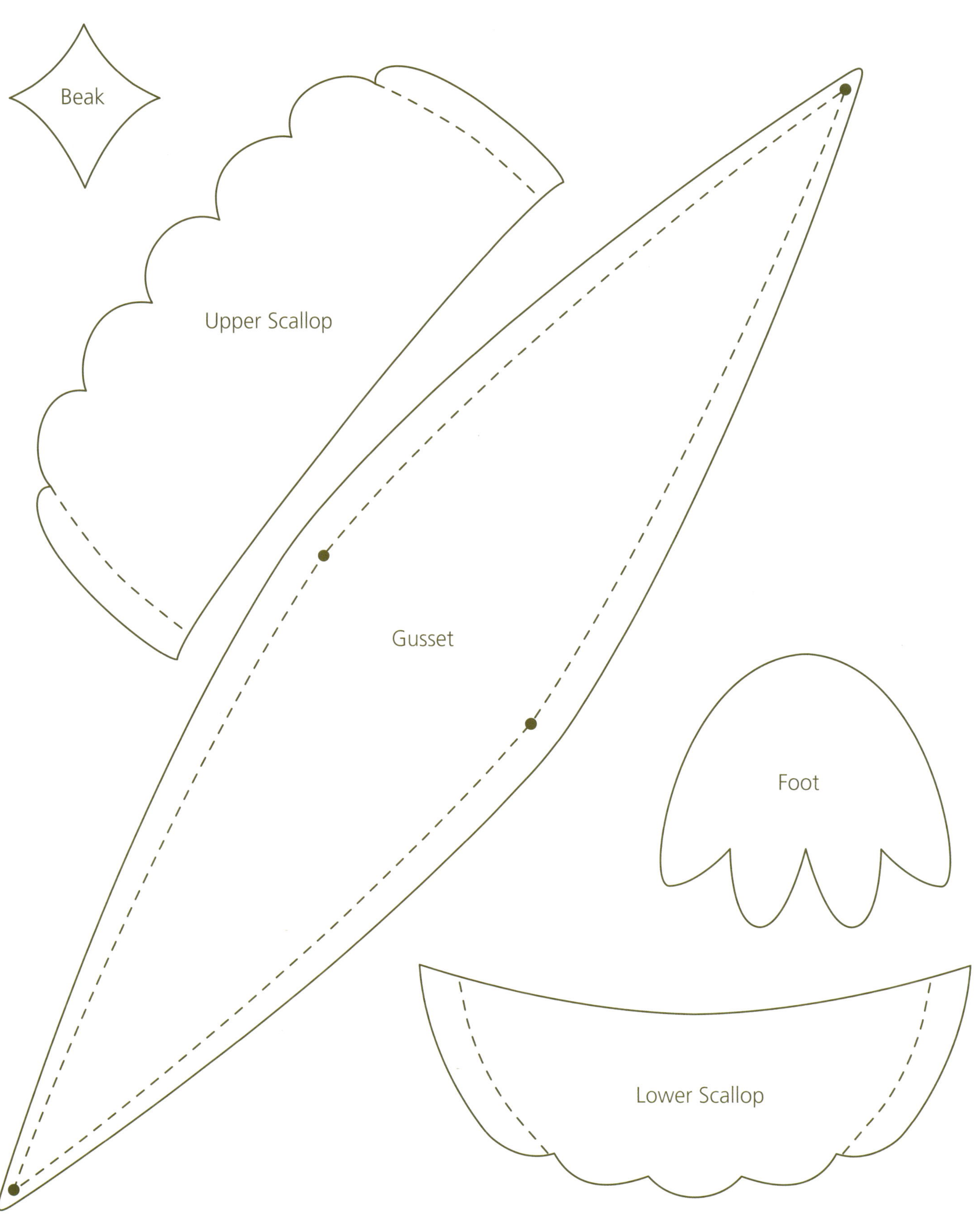
Beak
Upper Scallop
Gusset
Foot
Lower Scallop

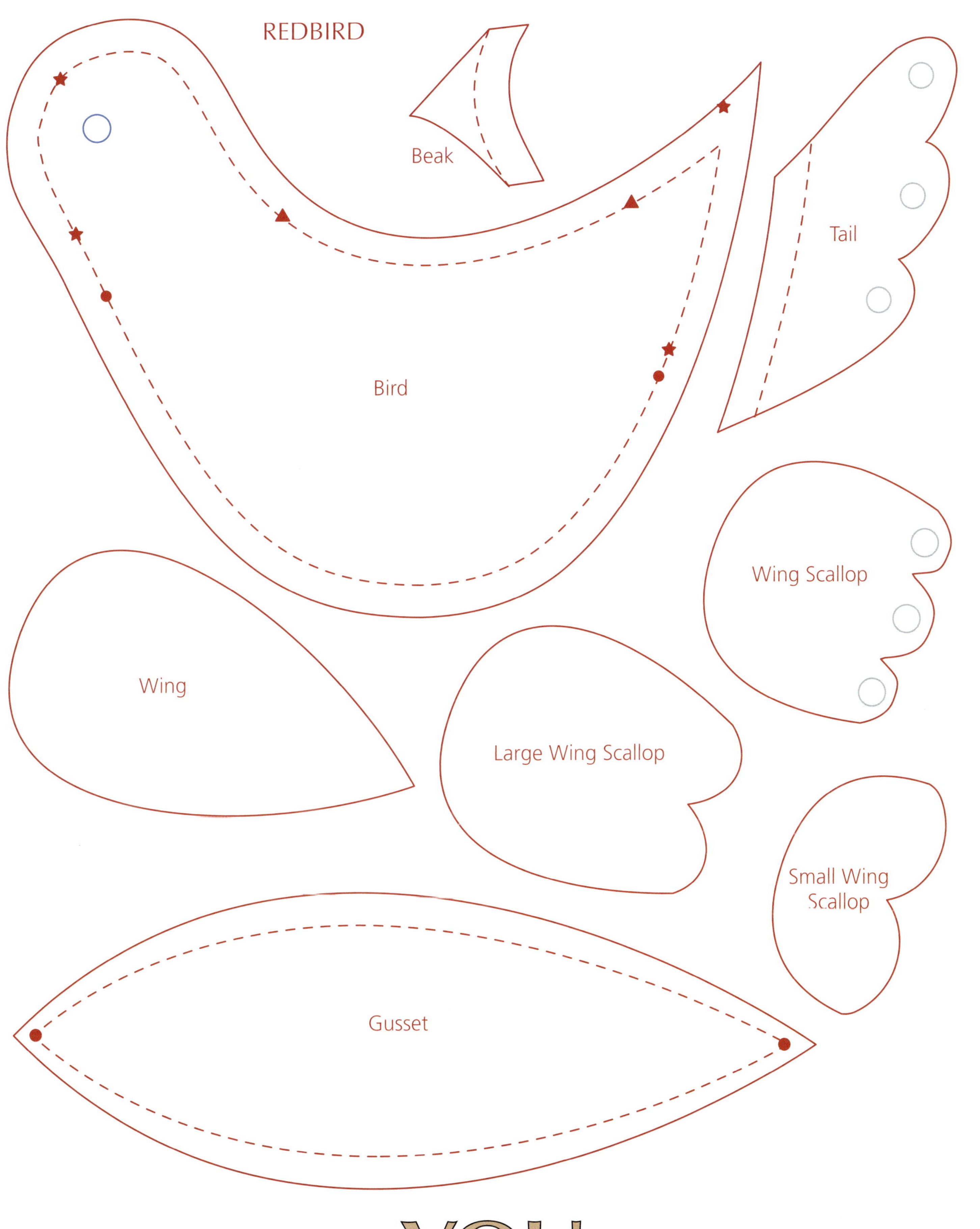
REDBIRD
Beak
Tail
Bird
Wing Scallop
Wing
Large Wing Scallop
Small Wing Scallop
Gusset

PERSONALIZED TRAY

WALL ART

Bud
Flower Center
Inner Petal
Bud Center
Outer Petal
Leaf
Stem
Middle Petal

tips and techniques

- Exclusively You Sheets of Smooth Faux Leather, Mock Croc, and Mock Snake measure 8½" x11". When the instructions refer to faux leather, this includes Smooth Faux Leather, Mock Croc, or Mock Snake. Shop for Exclusively You at your local retailer or online at www.TheLeisusureBoutique.com.
- For easy pattern making, trace the pattern onto tracing paper and cut it out. Place pattern face down on the wrong side of faux leather. Draw around pattern using a black ink pen on light colors and white marking pencil on dark colors. Cut out along drawn lines.
- Cut faux leather with utility scissors or a craft knife. You can also use a rotary cutter, ruler, and mat to cut pieces with straight edges.
- Use general purpose sewing thread and a heavy-duty sewing machine needle. Using a leather needle may make sewing through several layers of faux leather easier.
- Many machines sew easily through faux leather, but using a walking foot or Teflon coated presser foot may be helpful. Another option to help faux leather feed through the machine easier is to place tissue paper on either side of the faux leather (over the feed dogs and under the presser foot).
- Set your machine for a slightly longer stitch length. Use a ¼" seam allowance for all sewing unless otherwise noted in project instructions.
- If needed, finger-press faux leather. Do not use an iron on faux leather.
- Beacon® Fabri-Tac™ Permanent Adhesive works well to adhere faux leather pieces.
- To dry brush highlights and edges, lightly dip a clean dry brush into paint. Remove excess paint by wiping bristles on a paper towel. Using light stokes, apply the paint to the project.
- Painting the cut edges of faux leather pieces with coordinating acrylic paint will give your project a finished look.

Production Team: Designers – Anne Stocks, Becky Werle, and Kim Hamblin; Technical Editor – Lisa Lancaster; Technical Writer – Jean Lewis; Graphic Artists – Dana Vaughn and Jacob Casleton; Photography Stylist – Christy Myers.

We have made every effort to ensure that these instructions are accurate and complete. We cannot, however, be responsible for human error, typographical mistakes, or variations in individual work.